The BOYS' ChriStmaS book

PSS!
PRICE STERN SLOAN

An Imprint of Penguin Group (USA) Inc.

Written by Tracey Turner
Illustrated by Paul Moran

Cover illustrated by Andrew Geeson

Use common sense at all times—always wear appropriate safety gear,
be very careful with scissors, and be considerate of other people.

PRICE STERN SLOAN
Published by the Penguin Group
Penguin Group (USA) Inc., 375 Hudson Street, New York, New York 10014, USA
Penguin Group (Canada), 90 Eglinton Avenue East, Suite 700,
Toronto, Ontario M4P 2Y3, Canada
(a division of Pearson Penguin Canada Inc.)
Penguin Books Ltd., 80 Strand, London WC2R 0RL, England
Penguin Group Ireland, 25 St. Stephen's Green, Dublin 2, Ireland
(a division of Penguin Books Ltd.)
Penguin Group (Australia), 250 Camberwell Road, Camberwell, Victoria 3124, Australia
(a division of Pearson Australia Group Pty. Ltd.)
Penguin Books India Pvt. Ltd., 11 Community Center,
Panchsheel Park, New Delhi—110 017, India
Penguin Group (NZ), 67 Apollo Drive, Rosedale, Auckland 0632, New Zealand
(a division of Pearson New Zealand Ltd.)
Penguin Books (South Africa) (Pty.) Ltd., 24 Sturdee Avenue,
Rosebank, Johannesburg 2196, South Africa

Penguin Books Ltd., Registered Offices:
80 Strand, London WC2R 0RL, England

Copyright © 2010, 2011 Buster Books. First published in Great Britain as *The Boys' Christmas Book* and *The Boys' Rainy Day Book*
by Buster Books, an imprint of Michael O'Mara Books Limited. First published in the United States in 2012 by
Price Stern Sloan, a division of Penguin Young Readers Group, 345 Hudson Street, New York, New York 10014.
PSS! is a registered trademark of Penguin Group (USA) Inc. Manufactured in Singapore.

ISBN 978-0-8431-7197-6   10 9 8 7 6 5 4 3 2 1

CONTENTS

PUZZLES AND QUIZZES

Christmas World 5

Winter Races 6–7

Festive Family Fun 8–9

Candy Cane Game 11

Ride On 12–13

Christmas Code-Breakers 18–19

Robot Invasion 20–21

Elfish Antics 22–23

Merry Maze 25

Destination: North Pole 26–27

Animal Games 28

Santa Dash! 32–33

Colosseum Conundrums 34–35

Party Puzzlers 36–37

Untangle the Lights 40

Tricky Trees 49

Mountain of Doom 51

Snow-Doku 59

Fly Trap 62

Food, Glorious Food 64–65

Periscope Puzzler 68–69

Surprise! 74–75

Can You Save the Day? 76–77

True or False? You Decide! 82

Go-Kart, Go! 83

What's Your Ultimate Superpower? 86

STORY TIME

The Mystery of the Hungry Snow Monster 14–15

The Power of Christmas 81

THINGS TO DO

Reindeer Rules 10

Fly a UFO 16–17

Christmas Cheer 29

Be a Mathematical Mastermind 38–39

Cards that Pop! 41

Yummy Decorations 46–47

Reach into a Monster's Stomach 50

Design Your Own Dino Comic Strip 54–55

Build a Cool Camp 60–61

Christmas Obstacle Course 70–71

Make a Spyscope 72–73

Say Merry Christmas 84

Seasonal Scraps 88–89

GAMES TO PLAY

Mission: Secret Agent 30–31

Christmas Card Tricks 42–43

Timed Tabletop Test 44

Daring Dice-Off 52–53

Rooftop Ride 56–57

After-Dinner Games 66–67

Christmas Bingo 78–80

DOODLES TO DO

4, 7, 12, 24, 26, 34–35, 45, 48, 55, 58, 63, 65, 85, 87

ALL THE ANSWERS

90–96

Draw the perfect present.

CHRISTMAS WORLD

Christmas is celebrated in lots of different countries. Each one has its own weird and wonderful traditions, but can you guess which festive fact below is false? Check your answer on page 90.

FACT 1. In France, Santa Claus (who they call Père Noël) gives small presents to children on the night of December 6. He also gives out presents on Christmas Eve.

FACT 2. In Latvia, Santa Claus is even busier. He gives out presents on each of the 12 days of Christmas, starting on Christmas Eve.

FACT 3. According to Greek legend, the "Killantzaroi" are naughty goblins who come out at Christmas time. Burning a fire in the fireplace day and night for 12 days is believed to keep them away.

FACT 4. In Japan, Hotei-osho gives out gifts at Christmas. He is said to have eyes in the back of his head so he can see whether children have been good.

FACT 5. In Iceland, the "Jólasveinar" are 13 elflike creatures who get up to mischief before leaving presents in children's shoes at Christmas. They have names such as Sausage Snatcher, Door Slammer, and Pot Licker!

FACT 6. In Italy, as well as being brought presents from Santa Claus, children are also given gifts by a friendly witch called "La Befana."

FACT 7. In Ukraine, a family must watch out for the first evening star to appear in the night sky. Once they spot the star, Christmas dinner feasting can begin.

FACT 8. Mexican children take a swing at a piñata—a bright papier-mâché shape filled with sweets—and scoop up the Christmas treats that shower down from it.

FACT 9. In Great Britain, children traditionally hang stockings—large socks—from their front door for Santa Claus to fill with presents.

FACT 10. In Australia, Santa can sometimes be seen surfing the waves on Christmas Day.

WINTER RACES

Win the winter sports championship by completing these puzzles at record speed. All the answers are on page 90.

SNOWBOARDING CHAMP

Charlie the champion snowboarder has his goggles on. His snowboard has stripes on it, but no stars. Can you spot him?

SMART SKIERS

Only two of these skiers are exactly the same. Can you spot the identical pair?

BOBSLED RUN

Which bobsled is the only one to finish the race?

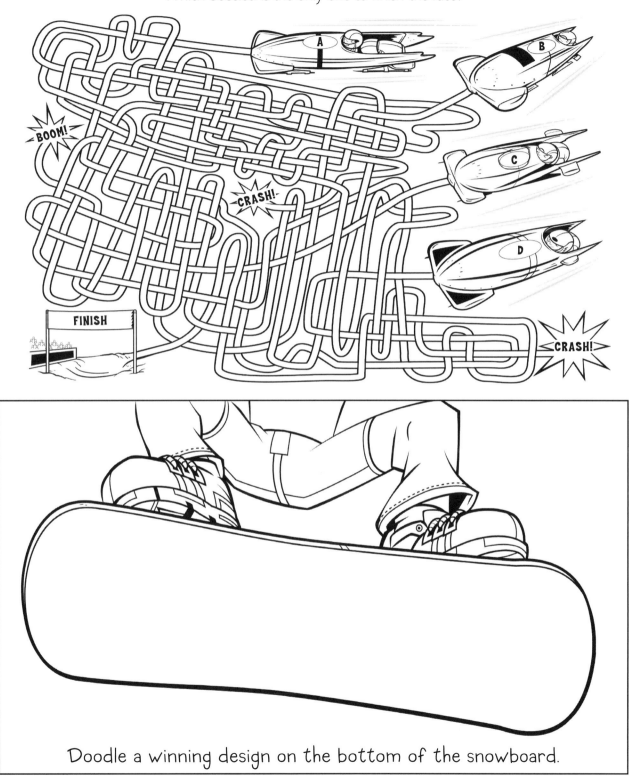

Doodle a winning design on the bottom of the snowboard.

FESTIVE FAMILY FUN

Play this Christmas quiz with your friends and family, and find out who are the real Christmas stars. Fill in each player's answers—A, B, C, or D—in the scoreboard on the opposite page.
Check the answers on page 90.

1. How do you wish someone "Merry Christmas" in Spanish?

- **A.** Joyeux Noël
- **B.** Buon Natale
- **C.** Feliz Navidad
- **D.** Prettige Kersydagen

2. What colors are traditionally associated with Christmas?

- **A.** Yellow and purple
- **B.** Pink and blue
- **C.** Red and green
- **D.** Orange and red

3. What is January 6 also known as?

- **A.** Twelfth Night
- **B.** The Feast of Stephen
- **C.** Boxing Day
- **D.** Mother's Day

4. Which method of transport is traditionally used by Santa Claus?

- **A.** Skis
- **B.** A sleigh pulled by reindeer
- **C.** A bobsled
- **D.** A white horse

5. In the song "The Twelve Days of Christmas," how many drummers drumming are there?

- **A.** three
- **B.** six
- **C.** nine
- **D.** twelve

6. Santa Claus is named after which saint?

- **A.** Santa Clarance
- **B.** Saint Nicholas
- **C.** Santa Clare
- **D.** Saint Christopher

7. What is a traditional Christmas song known as?

- **A.** A Christmas jingle
- **B.** A Christmas carol
- **C.** A Christmas ditty
- **D.** A Christmas shanty

8. When did the first Christmas cards go on sale?

- **A.** 1643
- **B.** 1743
- **C.** 1843
- **D.** 1943

9. In which country is Santa Claus known as Swiety Mikolaj?

A. France
B. Denmark
C. Syria
D. Poland

11. What color is Rudolph's nose?

A. Blue
B. Green
C. Pink
D. Red

10. Dasher, Dancer, Prancer, Vixen, Comet, Cupid, Donner, Rudolph, and … ?

A. Big Daddy
B. Bruiser
C. Blitzen
D. Byron

12. What type of tree is a traditional Christmas tree?

A. Evergreen fir
B. Oak
C. Sycamore
D. Chestnut

Question	Player One	Player Two	Player Three	Player Four
1				
2				
3				
4				
5				
6				
7				
8				
9				
10				
11				
12				
TOTAL SCORE				

REINDEER RULES

Copy the picture using the grid below and create your own Rudolph the reindeer.

CANDY CANE GAME

Can you spot the 20 candy canes hidden in this ski lodge?
All the answers are on page 90.

RIDE ON

If it's snowing too hard to try out your tricks in the skate park, why not try out some tricky puzzle moves instead? All the answers are on pages 90–91.

SKATER SKILLS

Check out these skaters, then answer the questions below:

A. How many skaters have backpacks on?

B. How many skaters are completely in the air?

C. How many skaters have only one arm in the air and have both feet on their skateboards?

D. How many skaters have crash-landed?

Design your own skateboard deck.

LAND THIS JUMP

Can you help skater Jim land this jump? There is only one square of pavement that is safe to land on, so you need to choose very carefully where you think Jim should land so that he doesn't fall off.

Clue: The level square is white. It is in a row with three gray squares and in a column with two black squares.

CHAIN REACTION

Some skaters use chains to make sure they don't lose their wallets while they're doing tricks, but these skaters' chains have become tangled up.

Can you follow the chains to figure out which wallet belongs to which skater?

THE MYSTERY OF THE HUNGRY SNOW MONSTER

Ben and Harry couldn't wait to open their presents on Christmas morning, but would they ever make it out alive from the depths of the dark woods?

Harry crept downstairs early on Christmas morning. Harry and his younger brother, Ben, were tired, but not because they had stayed up waiting for Santa's visit . . .

The boys had stayed up until after midnight listening to Grandfather. He had told them the legend of the hungry snow monster that lived in the big woods just behind their house. He had explained to them that the monster left the woods at dawn every Christmas in search of a feast.

As Harry tiptoed softly down the steps, he heard a rustling. *Ben had better not be opening the presents*, he thought.

He discovered the front door was wide open and the wind was blowing sheets of newspaper everywhere. Rushing to shut the door, Harry spotted Ben running through a thick blanket of snow. Harry rushed out to the garden, hopping as he tried to pull on his boots.

"Ben! What are you doing?" he shouted, but his brother didn't stop. Looking at the woods in the distance, Harry felt a shiver of fear run down his spine—he remembered his grandfather's story about the hungry snow monster . . . but although he was scared, he took a deep breath of icy air and ran after his brother.

The two of them tore off across a wide, white field together, leaving footprints in the freshly fallen snow.

As Harry caught up with Ben, he noticed another set of footprints— big footprints—which disappeared into the dark woods.

Ben stopped, puffing little clouds as he gasped for air. "It's Rufus," he panted. "I opened the door to look at the snow, and the silly puppy disappeared! We have to find him!"

They stared into the woods of gnarled, old trees and thick undergrowth. "Er, these footprints look a bit big for a puppy. They could belong to . . . to the—" Harry gulped. "The snow monster!"

Ben nodded nervously. Harry picked up a large stick and handed Ben a sharp icicle that had fallen from the branch of a tree.

The boys headed into the woods. Brambles tore at their clothes as they crunched along the dimly lit, narrow path.

There was no sign of Rufus anywhere, but the boys kept walking. It was eerily quiet, until the boys heard a fierce "ROAAAAAAR!"

Harry twirled around, stick at the ready. A set of razor-sharp teeth and beady eyes glowed from the mouth of a nearby cave.

"Ben!" whispered Harry, looking at the snow. "Paw prints. Puppy paw prints! Rufus must be in the monster's lair." How on Earth were they going to rescue him without becoming the snow monster's Christmas nighttime snack?

"*Grrrrrrrrrrrrrrrrr!*" The monster's growl echoed through the trees. Harry jumped in fright, throwing his stick into the air. Harry shut his eyes tightly as a dark, furry creature leaped out of the cave. The monster was attacking!

When Harry finally opened his eyes, Ben was on the floor, laughing hysterically. The beast had caught the stick and dropped it obediently at Harry's feet.

The "monster" in the cave turned out to be Cocoa—their friend's dog—and following in Cocoa's big paw prints was Rufus, safe and sound. Harry sighed in relief, "Come on, you bad dogs. Let's go home," he said.

As the boys reached their garden, they heard another roar. Had the snow monster found them? No. The sound was coming from just inside the fence.

"*Boooooys!* Where have you been?"

FLY A UFO

Unidentified Flying Objects, commonly known as UFOs, are one of the world's great mysteries. Some people believe these flying saucers could be alien aircraft. Find out how to make your own, then send it flying through the solar system on a cool alien adventure.

MAKE A UFO

You Will Need:

• an old Frisbee • a tennis ball
• silver duct tape • a black marker
• a large bowl • 8 pieces of
11 x 17 in. paper

1. Place the tennis ball in the middle of the top of the Frisbee and use a couple of strips of duct tape to hold it in place.

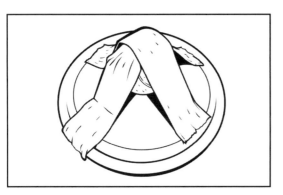

2. Continue wrapping strips of duct tape over the tennis ball and around the Frisbee until it is covered.

3. Use the marker to draw windows around the tennis ball part of your UFO.

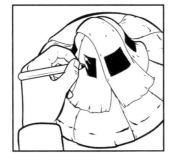

4. Throw your UFO as you would a Frisbee until you get the hang of it.

MAKE THE SOLAR SYSTEM

5. Draw around the bowl to create a circle on each piece of paper—these will represent the eight planets of the solar system.

6. Cut each circle out.

7. Write the name of a different planet in the solar system inside each circle.

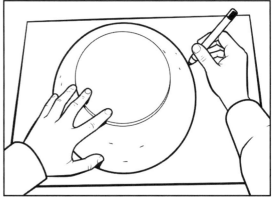

The names of the planets in the solar system are:

Mercury, Venus, Earth, Mars, Jupiter, Saturn, Uranus, and Neptune.

8. Arrange your planet circles in the above order in a line on the floor. Mercury is closest to the sun.

ALIEN GAME PLAY

You're now ready to launch your UFO into space and begin your alien adventure.

Your Mission: You have been informed by the head aliens on the mother ship that your UFO must land on each of the planets of the solar system in order.

Place the bowl at the bottom of the line of planets (this represents the sun) and stand with one leg on either side of the bowl.

Now throw the UFO so that it lands on Mercury.

If you're successful, retrieve the UFO and then throw it so that it lands on Venus. If you are unsuccessful, you must start again at Mercury.

Continue until you have visited each of the planets, always starting again at Mercury and visiting the planets in order if any of your throws are unsuccessful.

Why not time yourself to see how quickly you can complete your flight through the solar system? Good luck, alien explorer.

DID YOU KNOW?

For 76 years, Pluto was considered the ninth and smallest planet in the solar system. It lost its planet status in 2006 however, when it was reclassified as a "dwarf planet" because it was considered too small to be a real planet.

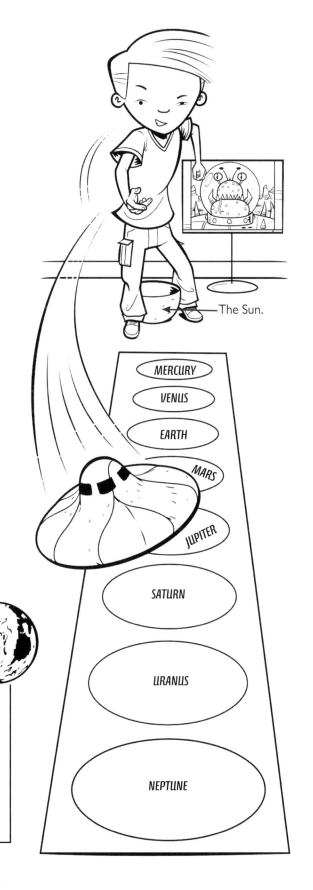

The Sun.

MERCURY

VENUS

EARTH

MARS

JUPITER

SATURN

URANUS

NEPTUNE

CHRISTMAS CODE-BREAKERS

Help Santa crack a cryptic wish list and solve a coded treasure hunt using these cool Christmas codes. All the answers are on page 91.

As every secret agent knows, a code is a way of hiding messages by replacing either whole words with a different word or individual letters with symbols, numbers, or different letters. The following codes scramble the alphabet to mask a message.

ADVENT ALPHABET CODE

To write this alphabet code, simply replace each letter in your message with the letter two places after it in the alphabet. For example, if you want to write an A, you need to count two letters along in the alphabet, so A becomes C. If you want to write Z, just start at the beginning of the alphabet again, so Z becomes B.

"MERRY CHRISTMAS" becomes "OGTTA EJTKUVOCU."

To make it even harder to decipher, take out the spaces between the words, or group the letters in threes or fours to confuse the reader. For example, OGTT AEJT KUVO CU.

CRYPTIC WISH LIST

Jim believes he's been especially good this year, so he thinks he can get away with playing a trick on Santa . . .

He has written his Christmas wish list in an alphabet code, but in his code, he jumped back six letters in the alphabet.

Can you help Santa to decode Jim's letter?

Dear Santa,

My ultimate Christmas wish list would be . . .

SUATZGOTHOQK

MGSKIUTYURK

YQGZKHUGXJ

From, Jim x

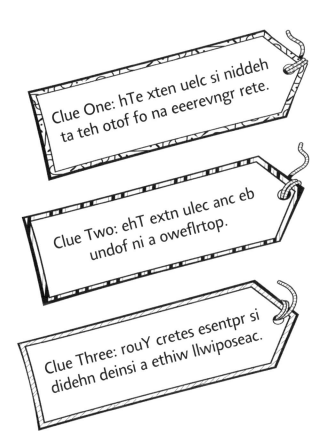

Clue One: hTe xten uelc si niddeh ta teh otof fo na eeerevngr rete.

Clue Two: ehT extn ulec anc eb undof ni a oweflrtop.

Clue Three: rouY cretes esentpr si didehn deinsi a ethiw llwiposeac.

SEASONAL SCRAMBLE CODE

This code scrambles up the letters in each word so that they don't make sense. For example:

"CHRISTMAS COOKIES" . . . becomes "CRHMASTIS OKOESIC."

Crack the clues opposite to discover where a secret present is hidden.

Why not set up your own treasure hunt using coded clues for your family on Christmas Day?

Hide the clues in advance, then hand out the first clue to get your family started. Don't forget to lead them to a hidden present—a bag of chocolate coins makes the perfect treasure.

CODED GIFT TAGS

Codes can also be made using numbers. For this code, you have to substitute each letter of the alphabet with a number that corresponds to its position in the alphabet. For example:

A = 1, B = 2, and so on.

Can you discover who these Christmas gifts are intended for?

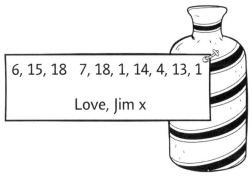

6, 15, 18   7, 18, 1, 14, 4, 13, 1

Love, Jim x

6, 15, 18   1, 21, 14, 20
19, 21, 19, 1, 14

Love, Jim x

6, 15, 18   18, 21, 6, 21, 19
20, 8, 5   4, 15, 7

Love, Jim x

ROBOT INVASION

It's the year 2050 and robots are taking over the Earth.
Solve the puzzles to defeat them, then turn
to page 91 to check your answers.

METAL MUNCH MIX-UP

This robot has been designed
to help you fight robot
enemies. He eats metal
and needs feeding before
he can help.

Can you complete the
contents of his stomach
so that each column, each
row, and each of the four
larger squares contains only
one coat hanger, one fork,
one phone, and one saucepan?

DOGBOT ATTACK

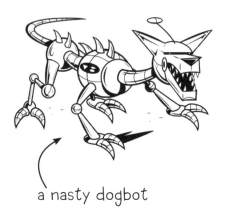

a nasty dogbot

The dogbots are attacking! They are all run from a central
computer, and to hack into it you will need to enter the
password 7, 3, 9, 4 in "binary code." Binary code is the
language that all computers use to process information.

The information is converted into ones (1) and zeros (0).
Can you work out the sequence of ones and zeros you
need to enter to stop the dogbots in their tracks?

DECIMAL	0	1	2	3	4	5	6	7	8	9	10
BINARY	0	1	10	11	100	101	110	111	1000	1001	1010

PARTS PANIC

Quick! You need to build a robot that will fight all the other robots before they break into the house.

Only one of these boxes contains all the parts you need to build the robot below. Can you figure out which box it is?

PROGRAMMER POWER

The letters opposite represent different types of robots. Each of the circles represents a robot power that has been programmed into its computer.

Where the circles cross over one another, the robots are programmed to do more than one thing. For example, robot J can walk forward and shoot lasers, and robot D can walk backward as well as sideways.

Can you spot the robot that can shoot lasers, walk sideways and forward, but can't walk backward?

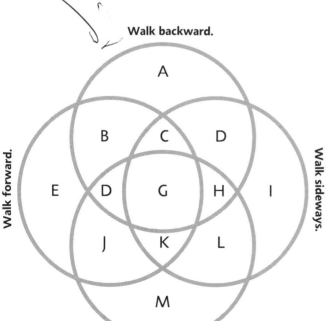

21

ELFISH ANTICS

Give Santa's little helpers a hand by solving the elves'
puzzling problems. All the answers are on page 91.

HIDDEN PRESENTS

Eric the Elf has lost six presents. Can you spot them and write down their coordinates?
To find the coordinates, write down the letter of the row and the number of the
column in which the item appears. For example, there is a toy pig in A1.

1. Toy soldier **2.** Phone **3.** Mini motorbike **4.** Toy car **5.** Toy robot **6.** Dinosaur

ALL WRAPPED UP

Finn the Forgetful Elf has forgotten what's inside these presents. Can you help him out?

1. Finn remembers that he wrapped the train set in wrapping paper with Christmas trees on. It also has a striped bow on it. Draw a circle around the present with the train set inside.

2. Finn knows that he wrapped the water pistol in paper that doesn't have any Christmas trees on it. It has a ribbon around it and no bow. Draw a square around the present with the water pistol inside.

BUILD THE TOY CAR

Elvis the Elf needs your help. One of these boxes contains all the pieces he needs to make this toy car, but he can't figure out which.

Can you help him?

A   B   C   D

Draw more presents on the conveyor belt.

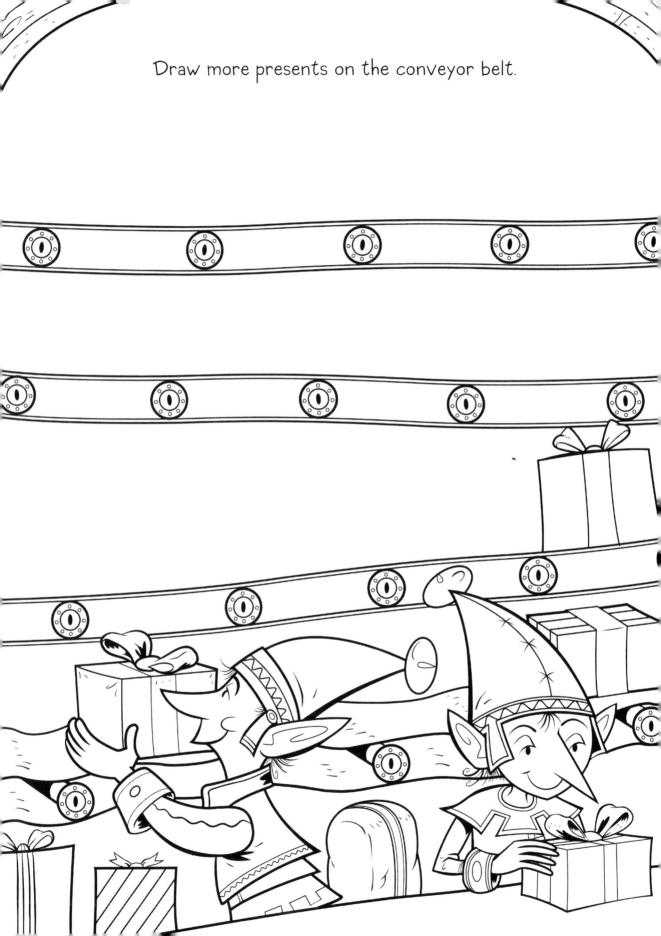

MERRY MAZE

Can you make your way from the entrance of the Santaland theme park to the workshop without passing any gifts? Once you've done this, can you make your way back out without passing any sacks? Check your route on page 92.

The Arctic

DESTINATION: NORTH POLE

Find out some freezing facts about where Santa Claus lives and make an igloo that won't melt! Read on to find out how.

POLE POSITION

• The North Pole is the most northerly point on planet Earth. There is no land there, just frozen sea ice that is 6½ to 10 ft. thick.

• No one lives at the North Pole, but people do live in the Arctic Circle—the area around the North Pole.

• The temperature at the North Pole varies between 32 °F in summer and –45 °F in winter.

• The North Pole spends half the year in darkness. The sun rises at the North Pole around March 21 and doesn't set again until around September 21. For the next six months, the pole is dark all day and night.

• There is a town in Alaska called North Pole with street names such as Santa Claus Lane and Saint Nicholas Drive. Its lampposts are even decorated to look like candy canes.

Draw more Arctic seals on the ice.

NORTH POLE PUZZLER:
Why don't polar bears eat penguins? The answer is revealed on page 92.

MARSHMALLOW IGLOO

You don't need any snow to make this igloo. Once you've finished it, display it in the middle of the Christmas dinner table for all to admire—and snack on!

You Will Need:

• a circle of white cardboard 6 in. in diameter • a large package of big marshmallows • 2⅓ cups of powdered sugar plus a handful for dusting
• 4 tablespoons of water • a knife

1. To build the bottom row of your igloo, place marshmallows around the edge of the circle of cardboard. Leave a 2 in. gap in the circle shape for the entrance.

2. Make a thick paste by mixing the powdered sugar with the water. This will be your "mortar" and will stick your marshmallow "bricks" together.

3. Spread some paste onto the base of a marshmallow and lay it, sticky side down, on top of two marshmallows as if you were laying a brick.

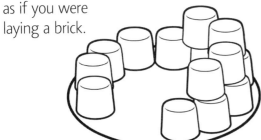

4. Repeat until you have made another row. Leave to dry for 20 minutes. Then lay one more row of marshmallow bricks and leave to dry for 20 minutes.

5. Next, pile marshmallows into the middle of your igloo until they start

coming out of the top. Cut a few marshmallows in half horizontally and use the paste to stick them to the top of your igloo to make a dome as shown above.

6. To make an arch, spread paste onto the bottom and side of one "brick" and place it on its side at the entrance. Make sure it sticks to the base and wall. Repeat on the opposite side. Add two more marshmallows on either side to build up the archway, then add a final marshmallow on top as shown here.

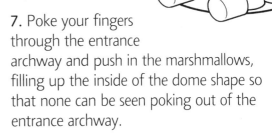

7. Poke your fingers through the entrance archway and push in the marshmallows, filling up the inside of the dome shape so that none can be seen poking out of the entrance archway.

8. Finally, dust your igloo with powdered sugar for a snow-drift effect and arrange some seasonal ornaments to create a snowy scene.

ANIMAL GAMES

These animals all live in or around the Arctic Circle, but not in the same place. Can you match the animals below to their names? The first one has been done for you. Check your animal knowledge on page 92.

A. Polar bear **B.** Wolverine **C.** Harp seal **D.** Arctic fox **E.** Arctic hare **F.** Walrus
G Musk ox **H.** Reindeer **I.** Narwhal **J.** Dall sheep **K.** Bowhead whale **L.** Arctic tern
M. Arctic puffin **N.** Arctic owl **O.** Arctic ground squirrel

CHRISTMAS CHEER

Impress your friends with these seriously cool Christmas drinks.
Each recipe makes four mocktails.

RED RUDOLPH SLURPER

Tell your friends the cherry is Rudolph's nose and
the wafers are his antlers!

You Will Need:

• 2/3 cup cola • 1/3 cup ginger beer • 4 scoops of strawberry
ice cream • 4 cherries • 8 wafers • a large bowl

Mix together the cola and ginger beer in a bowl, then divide the mixture into
four glasses. Add a round scoop of ice cream into each glass and stick a cherry
in the middle of the ice cream and a wafer on either side for antlers. *Voilà!*

SNOWBALL SPLAT!

Snowball cocktails are very popular at Christmas time. Here's
how to make a snowball mocktail that really packs a punch.

You Will Need:

• 1¼ cup lemon-lime soda • 1/3 cup lemon sorbet • squirt
of lemon juice • handful of crushed ice • a large flask or cocktail shaker

Put all the ingredients into the flask or cocktail shaker and shake up and down.
Pour into four glasses, then race your friends to drink it before it melts.

SLUSHY, MUSHY SURPRISE

Prepare to freeze with this seriously cool glass
of slushy, mushy mess.

You Will Need:

• 4 handfuls of crushed ice cubes • 1/3 cup
coconut milk • 3/4 cup pineapple juice
• a large flask or cocktail shaker

Put all the ingredients into the flask or cocktail
shaker and shake. Pour into four glasses and serve.

MISSION: SECRET AGENT

The CIA has been watching you and thinks you
might have what it takes to be its next secret agent.

All secret agents have to complete the recruitment mission below within
24 hours before being accepted by the CIA. Each task will test
a different aspect of your secret agent skills. Good luck!

SECRET AGENT SKILL 1: SECRECY

Your first task is to make your bedroom
into a safe base for your secret activities.
To do this, cut out a long strip of paper,
and write "Crime Scene Do Not Enter"
on it. Stick it across the door to your
secret base.

Next, think of a password and a secret
knock. Teach these only to those
people you trust to enter your secret
base. Make sure no one enters your
base without authorized permission
for 24 hours.

SECRET AGENT SKILL 2: STEALTH

Your second task is to demonstrate
your ability to disguise yourself and
sneak around without being noticed.
To do this, dress yourself in a disguise
consisting of a hat, a pair of sunglasses,
and a jacket.

Next, collect each item on the list opposite
from around the house, and get them back
to your secret base without being noticed.
If there is someone in one of the rooms
you need to enter, hide behind items of
furniture and carefully plan your mission
so as not to be seen.

You could, for example, make a loud noise
or call them from another room to draw
them out, and then sneak in while they're
not looking.

List of items to collect:
• a towel • a ruler • a bottle of shampoo
• a fork • a book
• a magazine • a bunch of keys

SECRET AGENT SKILL 3: ATTENTION TO DETAIL

As a secret agent you will be required to give detailed and accurate information to the CIA.

To demonstrate your ability to do this, cover the items you have collected in the previous task with the towel, then answer the following questions:

1. How many inches would you guess the length of the fork to be?

2. What brand of shampoo is it?

3. What is the title of the book?

4. How many keys are on the key ring?

5. What is on the front cover of the magazine?

Now, uncover your items and check your answers. Use the ruler to measure the length of the fork. (Your answer must be within 2 in.) You need at least four correct answers.

SECRET AGENT SKILL 4: BRAINPOWER

All the CIA's secret agents are given a code name. Crack the code below to find out what yours is.

Cigpv: Tckpuvqto

Clue: Move each letter two letters backward in the alphabet.

If you can figure it out and write the correct code name in the space provided on the ID card below, you will have access to the CIA. (Turn to page 92 to check that you have cracked the code correctly.)

Next, stick a photo or draw a picture of yourself in the box marked "Photo ID." Carefully cut out the card and keep it with you at all times.

Congratulations—you have now been accepted by the CIA and have qualified as a secret agent.

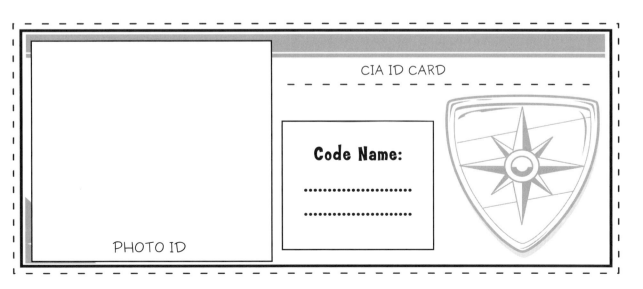

CIA ID CARD

Code Name:

....

....

PHOTO ID

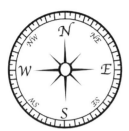

SANTA DASH!

Quick! Santa needs your help to deliver all of his presents in time. Turn to page 92 to see if you've been successful.

SANTA'S ADDRESS BOOK

Help Santa match the states to their capital cities in his address book. The first one has been done for you.

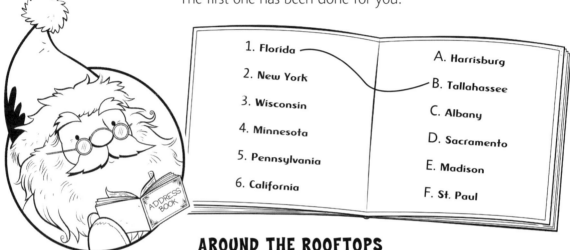

1. Florida
2. New York
3. Wisconsin
4. Minnesota
5. Pennsylvania
6. California

A. Harrisburg
B. Tallahassee
C. Albany
D. Sacramento
E. Madison
F. St. Paul

AROUND THE ROOFTOPS

Use the compass at the top of this page to help you work out which direction Santa is flying in. He flies north out of the chimney of house **A** until he reaches the last house in the village. He then flies east over four houses, then south over two houses. He then flies west over one house, and lands on the roof directly to the south of that house. Which roof does Santa end up on—**B** or **C**?

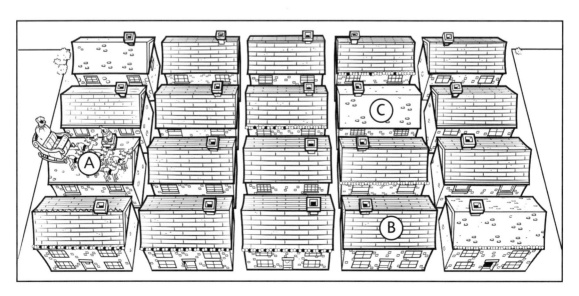

COMPASS CLUES

Use the compass on the opposite page to help Santa navigate his way around this village. Then answer the questions below.

1. Where is the tallest building in the village—in the north, south, east, or west?

2. What is immediately to the west of the village green?

3. What will the reindeer fly over to the northwest of the village?

4. Where is the largest group of houses Santa will visit?

5. What is immediately south of the shop?

6. How many houses will Santa visit in the northeast of the village?

Now see if your friends and family can do it from memory.

Let them study the map for two minutes, then cover it up and see how many questions they can answer correctly.

COLOSSEUM CONUNDRUMS

You're going to have to fight for your life to solve these puzzles! The answers are on page 93.

THIEF!

There is a thief somewhere in the crowd who has a beard, is wearing a brooch, and doesn't have a laurel wreath headdress. Can you spot him?

STATUE SPOTS

Can you spot ten differences between the statues of the Roman Emperor on the opposite page?

DID YOU KNOW?

The Colosseum was the name of the biggest games arena in Rome. It could seat up to 50,000 people. In the arena, many prisoners were forced to fight gladiators—men who were trained in deadly fighting techniques at special schools.

Give the gladiators swords and decorate their shields.

LOOK BEHIND YOU . . .

Gladiators were forced to fight wild beasts, including wolves, bears, and large cats. Connect the dots below to see what's behind the gladiator in time to warn him. Quick, before it's too late!

PARTY PUZZLERS

Get in the holiday spirit with these brain-tickling
puzzles and magical facts. Check your answers on page 93.

ODD HAT OUT

Each of these New Year's party hats has a pair . . . except one.
Can you spot the odd hat out?

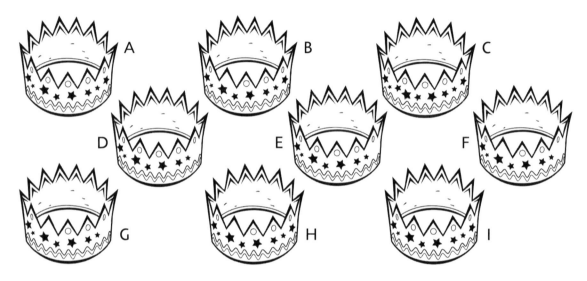

YULE LOGIC

Add a mocktail to the squares on the grid so that every chocolate "yule log" cake has at least one mocktail next to it horizontally or vertically, but not diagonally.

Beside each row and below each column is a number that tells you how many mocktails they should contain. No mocktail can be next to another mocktail, not even diagonally.

When every cake has a mocktail and all the numbers are correct, you've done it!

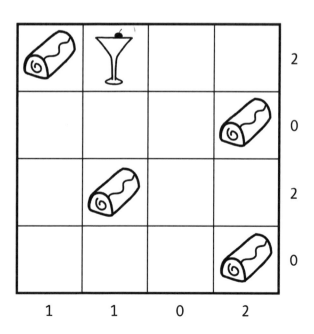

MISTLETOE DID YOU KNOW?

 Mistletoe is a plant with green leaves and white, poisonous berries that is traditionally hung up at Christmastime.

 The word "mistletoe" is thought to mean "dung on a twig." This is because mistletoe grows out of seeds found in birds' droppings.

 Ancient priests called "Druids" believed that mistletoe would bring good luck and health.

 In some countries, it is believed that kissing under a sprig of mistletoe will bring happiness to the couple.

MISTLETOE MYSTERY

There are 10 sprigs of mistletoe hidden in this party scene. Can you spot them all?

BE A MATHEMATICAL MASTERMIND

Use mathematics to read your friends' minds, impress your parents or teachers with lightning-speed calculations, and even guess their ages using the power of sums! You don't need to be a genius to be a mathematical mastermind, you just need to know these tricks.

MIND READER

Give a friend the following instructions:

1. "Choose a number—any number."

2. "Double it."

3. "Add ten."

4. "Divide it by two."

5. "Subtract your original number from the new one."

Then place your hands on your friend's head and close your eyes as if you are reading his mind. The secret of this trick is that the answer is always five! He will be amazed when you correctly guess the number he was thinking of.

THE MAGIC NUMBER

For this trick you will need a pen and five pieces of paper.

• On the first piece of paper, write the following numbers:

> 1, 3, 5, 7, 9, 11, 13, 15, 17, 19, 21, 23, 25, 27, 29, 31

• On the second piece, write the following numbers:

> 2, 3, 6, 7, 10, 11, 14, 15, 18, 19, 22, 23, 26, 27, 30, 31

• On the third piece, write the following numbers:

> 4, 5, 6, 7, 12, 13, 14, 15, 20, 21, 22, 23, 28, 29, 30, 31

• On the fourth piece, write the following numbers:

> 8, 9, 10, 11, 12, 13, 14, 15, 24, 25, 26, 27, 28, 29, 30, 31

• On the fifth piece, write the following numbers:

> 16, 17, 18, 19, 20, 21, 22, 23, 24, 25, 26, 27, 28, 29, 30, 31

You are now ready to start the trick. First, lay out the five pieces of paper on a table. Ask a friend to think of a number between 1 and 31.

Next, ask him to point to each piece of paper that has the number on it.

To find the correct number, simply add together the smallest number on each piece of paper that is pointed to.

For example, if his number was 11, he would point to the first, second and fourth pieces of paper.

The smallest numbers on each of those are 1, 2, and 8. 1 + 2 + 8 = 11, which is the number that he was thinking of.

GUESS SOMEONE'S AGE

Claim that you can guess anyone's age with the power of calculation. Simply ask the questions below to find out how. This trick only works if the person is ten or over. (Watch out for sneaky people lying about their age, too!)

1. Ask the person to multiply the first number of his or her age by five.

2. Ask him or her to add three to this figure.

3. Ask him or her to double it.

4. Ask the person to add the second number of his or her age to this figure. Ask him or her to tell you this number.

5. Take six away from the number that he or she has told you in step **4.** The number you end up with should be the person's age.

43×68+9÷214+73×2÷

Lightning-Speed Calculation

There's a quick way to check if a number can be divided exactly by three. Simply add up all the digits, and if they come to 3, 6 or 9, the number can be divided by three.

For 81, 8+1=9, so 81 can be divided by three. For 43, 4+3=7, which means 43 can't be divided by three.

The trick even works for huge numbers such as, 22,358,892. 2+2+3+5+8+8+9+2=39, 3+9=12, 1+2=3, so 22,358,892 can be divided by three.

GRAN . . . 27?

UNTANGLE THE LIGHTS

Untangle these lights to find which plug connects to the broken bulb. Check your answer on page 94.

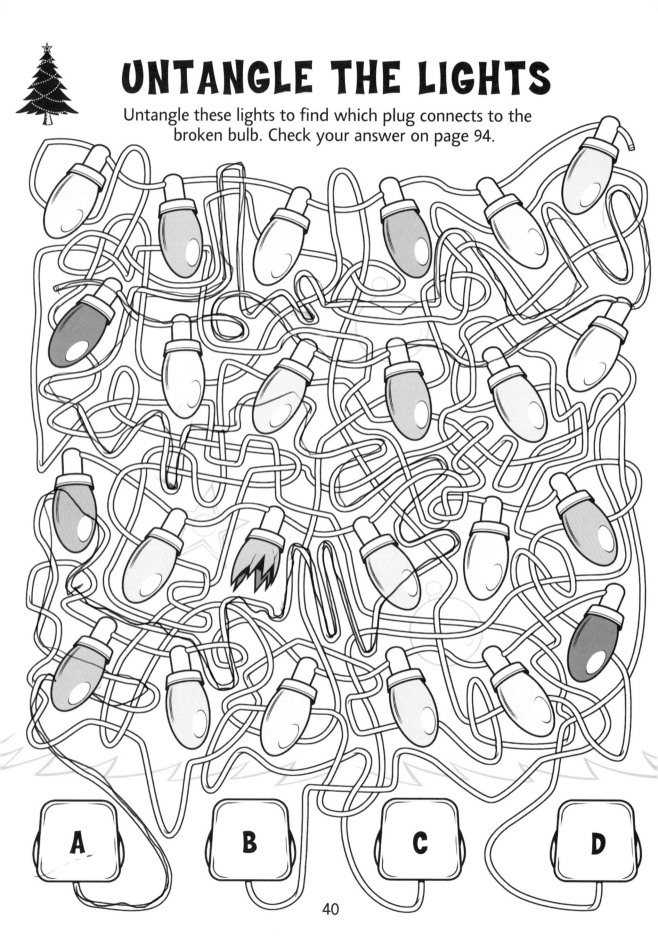

A   B   C   D

CARDS THAT POP!

Show off your card-making skills with these cool poppin' cards.

You Will Need:

- 3 sheets of 8½ by 11 in. card stock • scissors • pencil • glue stick • ruler

1. Fold two sheets of card stock in half widthwise.

2. On one of the folded cards, make four straight cuts—roughly 2 in. long, cutting from the folded edge of the card inward as shown below. These are the two flaps that will make your card "pop."

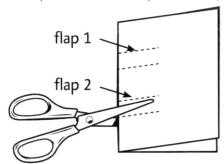

flap 1

flap 2

3. Unfold the cut piece of card, then push each of the flaps out so they form a right angle, as shown here.

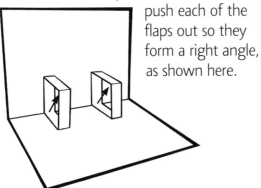

4. Draw two Christmas tree shapes on one of the other sheets of card. They should be 3 in. tall and 2 in. wide. Cut the trees out.

DID YOU KNOW?

The first Christmas cards ever sold were made in 1843 in England. Only 1,000 of them were made, and they were sold for sixpence.

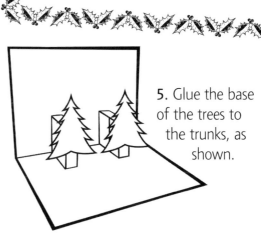

5. Glue the base of the trees to the trunks, as shown.

6. Leave to dry completely, then shut the card.

7. Glue the other piece of folded card onto the inner card, as shown below. Do not get any glue over the cutout areas.

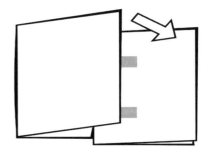

8. When your card is completely dry, write your Christmas greetings inside and give it to someone special.

CHRISTMAS CARD TRICKS

Perfect these amazing card tricks, then put on some magical after-dinner entertainment for friends and family.

WE FOUR KINGS

Before you perform this trick, you will need to set it up. Here's how:

• Remove all the aces and kings from an ordinary deck of cards.

• Place the four aces and four kings on top of the rest of the deck.

CARDS AT THE READY

1. Hand the pack to a volunteer in the audience and ask them to start dealing the cards facedown into two piles.

2. When they are about halfway through the deck, tell them to stop.

3. Put the undealt half of the pack to one side.

4. Ask them to split each of the two smaller piles into two even smaller piles in the same way. There should now be four piles of cards on the table.

5. Announce to your audience that you can tell just by looking at the piles that the top card on each pile is a king.

6. Next, ask your volunteer to turn the top card of each deck over so everyone can see it. You should have found all four kings!

7. Now tell the volunteer that you're "a real ace" at magic tricks . . . flip over what is now the top card on each of the four decks to reveal all the aces!

8. Take a bow.

THE TELEPORTING ACE

This trick is all about confidence—if you can convince your audience of something when it's not true, it's a breeze!

Before performing this trick, you will need to find the ace of diamonds in the deck of cards and hide it under the Christmas tree.

SHOWTIME!

1. Hold the pack of cards in one hand and tell the audience that you're going to do a trick using the first three aces you come across in the pack.

2. Making sure that the audience cannot see the cards in your hand, sift through the cards and call out which cards you are finding. However, when you reach the ace of hearts card, say "ace of diamonds" instead.

3. Once you have extracted the three aces from the pack, hide the ace of hearts in the middle of the three cards.

Fan them out so that the audience can't see which ace is in the middle, as shown. They will think that the ace of hearts is the ace of diamonds.

4. Put the cards back anywhere in the pack and give them a good shuffle.

5. Hand the pack of cards to a volunteer in the audience. Tell the audience that you are about to magically teleport one of the aces under the Christmas tree.

6. Pretend to use your teleporting skills. Put your head in your hands and frown.

7. Now ask the volunteer to go through the pack and pick out the aces. They will discover that the ace of diamonds is missing!

8. Tell the volunteer to take a look under the tree and soak up the magical glory.

TIMED TABLETOP TEST

To take this tabletop test, you will need a wristwatch (with a second hand), a table, a coin, and a mug. Use the second hand to time how long it takes you to complete all three parts of the test, and write your scores in the chart below. Then try to beat your own top time!

Before you begin, place the mug so that it is one hand span from the edge of the table, and place the coin so that it is touching the edge, as shown below. Now you are ready to begin the challenges.

Then catch it between your thumbs before it falls, as shown here:

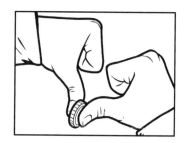

CHALLENGE 3

Still holding the coin between your thumbs, move your hands to the edge of the table by the mug.

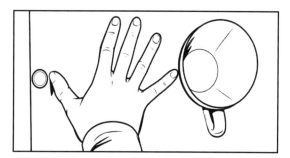

CHALLENGE 1

The aim of this challenge is to flick the coin around the mug until it is touching or hanging over the opposite edge of the table.

Use only your index finger to flick the coin. If you accidentally flick the coin off the table, start again. Don't push or drag the coin—that's cheating! You can use as many flicks as you like to complete the challenge.

Use your thumbs to throw the coin into the mug to complete the challenge.

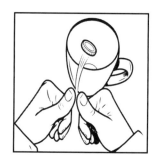

SCORE CHART

Write your times in the chart below:

CHALLENGE 2

This challenge takes skill and accuracy. First, spin the coin on its edge like so:

	Total Time
1st Attempt	
2nd Attempt	
3rd Attempt	

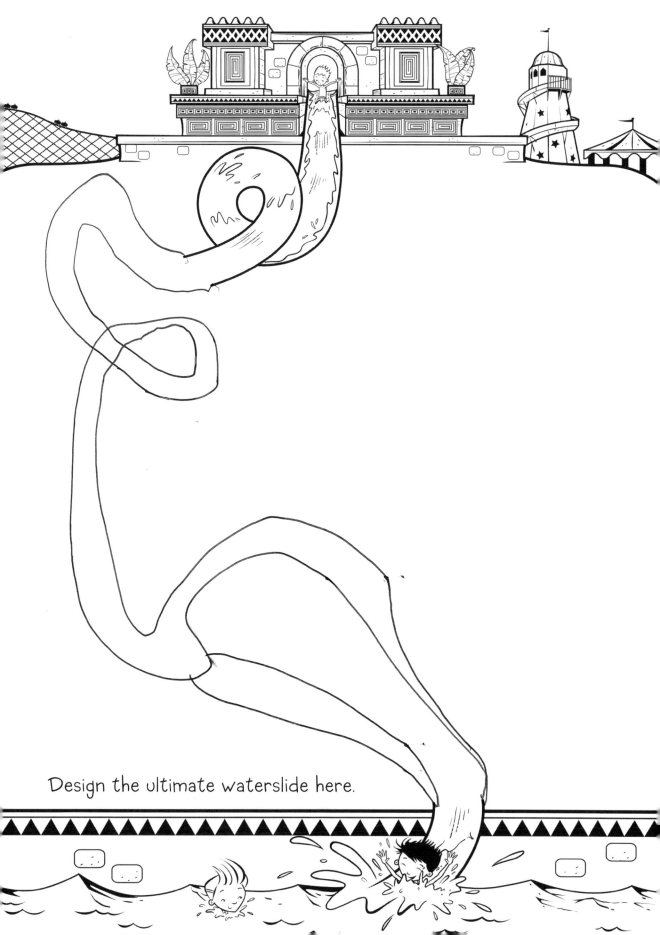

Design the ultimate waterslide here.

YUMMY DECORATIONS

Make these yummy, festive decorations and see how many make it on to the tree and not into your tummy.

GINGERBREAD MEN

You Will Need:

- tracing paper
- plastic wrap
- ribbon
- 3½ tablespoons superfine sugar
- 5 tablespoons softened butter
- 2 eggs
- 3½ tablespoons corn syrup
- 1 teaspoon baking powder
- 1 cup sifted flour
- 2 tablespoons ground ginger
- 1 teaspoon ground cinnamon
- a tube of ready-made icing

1. Place the tracing paper over the gingerbread man on the left and trace the outline. Cut it out and put it to one side.

2. Cream the butter and sugar together in a bowl.

3. Add the eggs, baking powder, and corn syrup and mix well.

4. Stir in the flour, ginger, and cinnamon and mix well until it forms a dough.

5. Place the dough in plastic wrap and chill it in the fridge for half an hour.

6. Ask an adult to preheat the oven to 350 °F.

7. Sprinkle some flour onto a clean surface then roll out the dough until it is about 1/4 in. thick.

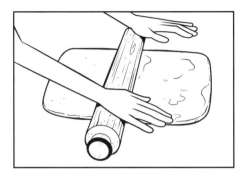

8. Place the traced outline of the gingerbread man on top of the dough and carefully cut around it with a knife.

9. Repeat until you have lots of gingerbread men and no dough left.

10. Place the gingerbread shapes on a greased baking tray and put it in the oven for 10 minutes or until they are golden brown.

Warning: Ask an adult to help you when using the oven.

11. When the gingerbread men are completely cool, give each one eyes, a mouth, a bow tie, and three buttons using the tube of ready-made icing.

12. Tie ribbon around their necks and hang them on the tree.

POPCORN GARLANDS

You will need a bowl of unsalted, unbuttered popcorn, a needle, and a length of red or green thread, roughly 3 ft. long.

Pierce pieces of popcorn with the needle and push them onto the thread. When you have a full garland of popcorn pieces, secure both ends with a double knot.

Hang your popcorn garland over the tree and feel free to take a nibble.

Christmas is celebrated all over the world.

Give these riders sleds . . .

. . . and give the surfers festive wet suits and Santa hats.

TRICKY TREES

There are 15 differences between these two pictures. Can you spot them all? The solution is on page 94.

REACH INTO A MONSTER'S STOMACH

. . . if you dare! First, make the monster below, then challenge members of your family to reach into his stomach to guess what he has eaten.

To make the monster, you will need:

• some old newspaper • a large cardboard box • a large piece of card stock • a pencil • scissors • paints • glue

1. Draw a monster's face on the piece of card stock. The monster should have a large, open mouth with big teeth.

2. Cut out a circle inside the monster's mouth so that there is a hole big enough to fit your hand inside.

3. Carefully cut around the outline of the head.

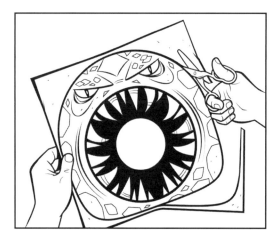

4. Lay the newspaper down on a table, then paint your monster, making him as scary-looking as possible. Leave to dry completely.

5. Carefully cut a hole that is as big as your monster's mouth on one side of the box.

6. Glue the monster face to the side of the box so that the monster's mouth is directly over the hole. Paint the outside of the box and leave to dry.

HOW TO PLAY

• Each player must choose three different items that will feel gross to touch from around the house, for example, peeled grapes or a slimy bar of soap would work well.

• Take turns placing the items in the box and challenge the other players to reach into the monster's stomach.

• Each player then has to guess what the monster has had for his dinner using only one hand. The player who guesses the most items correctly wins.

MOUNTAIN OF DOOM

The monster that lives on the Mountain of Doom has been terrifying the town. Can you find your way through the mountain to defeat him at the other end?

Be warned—if your path is blocked by venomous snakes, you cannot pass. You must pass over only one pack of dynamite and one flamethrower on your way. Turn to page 94 for help if you get lost. Quick, he's waking up!

DARING DICE-OFF

Challenge the family to the ultimate dice-off with these cool dice games.

DICE DECIDER

You Will Need:

- a pair of dice
- 3 or more players

Each player takes turns throwing the dice, then follow the instructions next to the number he or she has thrown.

TWO: Give someone in the house a piggyback ride.

THREE: Wear a Christmas decoration all day.

FOUR: Eat three Christmas cookies without drinking anything.

FIVE: Stand on your head and count to 20.

SIX: Make a drink for everyone.

SEVEN: Swap an item of clothing with the person next to you.

EIGHT: Do ten sit-ups, then five push-ups.

NINE: Sing a Christmas song.

TEN: Do a cartwheel, then a somersault.

ELEVEN: Recite the names of Santa's reindeer.

TWELVE: Do a silly dance for one minute.

SNOWMAN ROULETTE

You Will Need:

- 1 dice • 3 or more players • a pen and piece of paper for each player

1. Take turns rolling the dice. Each player has one chance to roll the dice per round.

2. Players must throw a "one" to begin. This allows them to draw the snowman's body, like the one shown.

3. Players must then wait until it is their turn again to try to roll a "two" to draw the head, and so on.

SCORING
Body = One
Head = Two
Hat = Three
Nose = Four
Eyes and Mouth = Five
Arms = Six

Each part of the snowman's body must be drawn in sequence, i.e., 1, 2, 3 etc.

4. The first player to complete his drawing of the snowman in the correct order wins.

CALL MY BLUFF!

This game is all about bluffing! The aim is to beat the previous player with a higher score . . . or bluff that you have.

You Will Need:

- 3 dice and an opaque, plastic cup
- 3 or more players

1. To start, Player One shakes the dice in the cup while covering the top of the cup with his hand.

2. Player One should then slam the cup down on the table and take a peek at the dice without anyone else seeing.

3. Player One must then decide to either tell the truth about the number that is rolled or to bluff.

For example, if Player One has rolled a low score, such as three, they might decide to bluff that they have rolled something higher, such as nine.

If Player One rolled a low score, they could tell the truth because there is no previous score to beat.

4. Player Two then has to guess if Player One is bluffing or not.

- If Player Two says, "BLUFF," the cup has to be lifted. If Player One was bluffing, Player One is out of the game.

- If Player Two says, "TRUTH," the cup doesn't have to be lifted and the dice and cup are passed to Player Two.

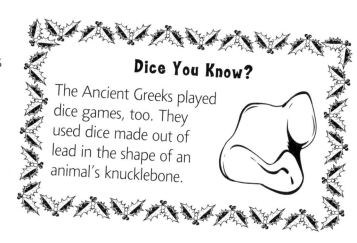

Dice You Know?

The Ancient Greeks played dice games, too. They used dice made out of lead in the shape of an animal's knucklebone.

5. Next, Player Two shakes the dice in the cup and slams it down on the table.

Player Two's score must beat Player One's score, so if it doesn't, Player Two will need to bluff a higher score.

6. Play continues until all but one player is out—they are the winning bluffer.

DESIGN YOUR OWN DINO COMIC STRIP

Learn how to draw Toby the T. rex, then make him the star of your own comic-book adventures.

To draw Toby, follow the instructions below. Try drawing him on scrap paper before starring him in the comic strips opposite.

You Will Need:

- scrap paper • a pencil • a black pen
- an eraser • some felt-tip pens

1. Use a pencil to draw rough ovals to show Toby's head and body. Add two lines coming to a point for his tail.

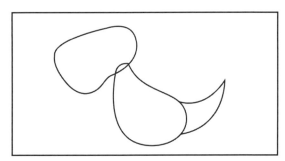

2. Add lines for his arms, legs, and feet, copying the shapes shown below as closely as you can.

3. Draw an *M* shape for Toby's eyes, then draw his mouth and claws in pencil. Go over your final lines with the black pen.

4. Draw in triangles for his teeth and circles for his eyeballs. Wait for the pen to dry, then erase all the pencil lines. Use the felt-tip pens to complete your picture of Toby.

Now that you have drawn Toby the T. rex, make him feature in your very own dino comic strip on the opposite page. Will he escape the nasty dinosaur and live to tell the tale?

THE ADVENTURES OF TOBY THE T. REX

WHAT HAPPENS NEXT? YOU DECIDE!

ROOFTOP RIDE

Santa needs you and your friends to help him deliver presents this year, so harness the reindeer and get ready for a rooftop tour around the world.

Each player must place a coin or counter on the "Start & Finish" square. Take turns spinning the spinner and moving your counter, then follow the instructions on the square you land on. The first player to make it back to Santa's Workshop wins.

A gust of wind helps you on your way. Move forward two squares.

Santa gets stuck in a chimney! Miss a turn.

The reindeer have an extra burst of speed. Move forward two squares.

Santa's spotted a shortcut. Move forward four squares.

Oh no! The sleigh has crashed into a telephone pole! Miss a turn to repair any damages.

Tailwinds blow the sleigh forward. Move forward four squares.

CRASH!

Rudolph slips on a roof tile and needs to rest his hoof. Miss a turn.

SANTA'S WORKSHOP
START & FINISH

Some presents fall out of the sleigh. Miss a turn to collect them.

Carrots left out for the reindeer make them gallop faster. Spin again.

SPINNER

1 2 3 4 5 6

Cut out this spinner and stick a toothpick through the middle. To spin it, hold the toothpick upright with one hand, and spin the spinner with the other. The number at the top of the spinner when it stops tells you the number of spaces you should move.

Design Santa the ultimate supersleigh.

SNOW-DOKU

Sid the Snowman has four picture grids. Can you complete the grids so that the columns and rows and the four smaller squares each contain only one of the items listed beneath it?

You can check your answers on page 94.

a carrot, a shovel,
a hat, and a lump of coal

a scarf, a snowman,
a holly leaf, and Santa's hat

a robin, a snowflake,
a glove, and a boot

a tree, a star,
a candle, and a twig

BUILD A COOL CAMP

Be the king of the castle and make the coolest camp
out of stuff you can find lying around the house.

RECONNAISSANCE MISSION

Identify a table or a desk
to form the anchor—the
basic structure—for your
cool camp.

BUILDING WORK

Position chairs all around
the anchor, then tie
scarves from the tops of
the chairs to the top joints
of your anchor, as shown below.
The scarves act as the support beams
for the camp.

Position large cushions around the
chairs to build up the walls, then drape
sheets and blankets over the entire
camp structure.

FAKE ENTRANCE

Fool intruders by making a fake
entrance to your camp. On one side of
the camp, place a few large cardboard
boxes in two rows, leaving a gap large
enough for a person to crawl through
in between the rows.

Drape a sheet over the
boxes as shown above,
and pin the ends
of this sheet
underneath the
corners of the
boxes closest to
your camp. This
will create a "sheet
wall" between the
fake tunnel and your
camp. Pile a second wall
of cushions behind the sheet
wall to block the pathway of
an intruder.

Place a sign saying "Tunnel Entrance" in front of the fake tunnel.

Now, make a real entrance on the other side of your camp by simply removing a wall of cushions to make a space between two chairs big enough to crawl through. Make sure no one sees you using the real entrance.

SOFT-TOY CANNONBALLS LAUNCH AREA

Find as many soft toys as you can and bring them into the fort. If you hear someone breaking their way through the tunnel, launch the soft toys at the enemy until he or she retreats.

Make sure there is also an area between the chairs on each side of your camp where you can fold back the sheets and blankets to create a hole big enough to throw soft toy cannonballs at intruders breaking in on any side.

STICKY TRAPS

Further secure your fort by placing booby traps along the tunnel. To do this, crawl halfway along the tunnel and lie on your back. Dangle strips of tape from the sheet roof of the tunnel so that the sticky side will hit intruders in the face.

ACQUIRE SUPPLIES

Supply your camp with the following special equipment:

- sleeping bags
- pillows and comfy cushions
- warm blankets
- a flashlight
- tape (for resetting booby traps)
- a notebook and pens
- binoculars
- cool stuff, for example your skateboard, books, and magazines
- snacks and drinks
- a dustpan and brush for keeping your camp clean of crumbs

Now kick back and enjoy being the king of your castle! Remember to keep your eyes and ears open for intruders.

FLY TRAP

Follow the cobweb lines to work out which spider has trapped which fly.
The answer is on page 94.

Design a superhero outfit to conceal your true identity.

FOOD, GLORIOUS FOOD

Christmas is a time for feasting, so get sucked into these mouthwatering puzzles. Check your answers on page 94.

DIFFERENT DINNERS

Match the traditional Christmas foods to their countries below.
The first one has been done for you.

1. Curried goat

2. Roast turkey with cranberry sauce

3. Pickled herring

4. Roasted eel

5. Dried shark

6. Orange, grapefruit, and radish salad

A. Italy

B. Jamaica

C. Iceland

D. Mexico

E. United Kingdom

F. Sweden

STORE DASH

Your family is missing some key ingredients for Christmas dinner, so you've been sent to the store.

The first thing on your list is sold in a store that isn't at either end of the street. The store isn't next door to a store that sells food or stamps. Do you buy some meat, vegetables, or sweets?

You buy your first item and go in the store opposite. Then you come out and turn left and buy something from the store next door. Do you buy stamps, sweets, or cheese?

You come out, turn right and buy another item from the shop two doors down. Do you buy bananas, bread, or flowers?

CANDY STORE CHALLENGE

You have 300 pennies left in your wallet. You want to buy 10 sugar mice for your Auntie Margaret's Christmas present. How many chocolate bars can you buy with the change? Alternatively, with the change, if you bought 1 gingerbread cookie, 2 candy canes, and 8 gumdrops, how many chocolate bars would you then be able to buy? (You may still go home with some pennies left in your wallet!)

Gingerbread cookies 10 ¢

Sugar mice 5 ¢

Chocolate bars 20 ¢

Candy canes 15 ¢

Gumdrops 2 ¢

What would you like for Christmas dinner?

AFTER-DINNER GAMES

If you're too full to move after stuffing your face with Christmas dinner, why not play these fun after-dinner games? You don't even have to move!

IN MY STOCKING I FOUND . . .

1. Players must take turns adding something to a list of imaginary items they found in a stocking.

2. The first player starts off the game by saying, "In my Christmas stocking, I found . . ." and then chooses an item that he found there. For example, " . . . a sports car." You can include anything—the funnier the better.

3. The next person must repeat the whole list then add another item.

4. Any player who forgets an item while repeating the list is out.

The game continues until one player remains.

SPOT THE LIE

1. Players take turns announcing two true statements about themselves and one statement that is a lie.

For example, "I know all the words to the song 'Jingle Bells,' I once ate a worm, and my favorite ice cream is blueberry."

2. Everyone else must decide which statement they think is a lie. If no one guesses the lie, the player wins one point.

3. The player with the most points after everyone has had two turns wins.

CRAZY CHRISTMAS DESIGNS

1. Give each player a piece of paper and a pencil.

2. Players must then draw 20 small dots anywhere on their paper—the more randomly spaced the better.

3. Once each piece of paper has the correct number of dots on it, gather them together and shuffle.

4. Hand each player a piece of paper.

5. Players then have one minute to connect the dots up to make the silliest Christmas-themed picture.

6. When the minute is up, all artwork must be displayed and voted on.

The player whose picture is awarded the most votes wins.

Rudolph X

CHRISTMAS NAME GAME

1. Each player must think of a famous Christmas character from a Christmas film, book, or song for the player on his or her right. Don't say it out loud.

Here are some character ideas: Scrooge or Tiny Tim from Charles Dickens' novel *A Christmas Carol*, an elf, Frosty the Snowman, one of Santa's reindeer, the Grinch.

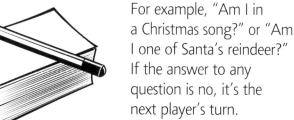

2. Write the name down on a sticky note and stick it on the player to your right's forehead. Make sure the player whose head the note is on can't see it.

3. The youngest player goes first. They have to guess the name on their forehead by asking questions with yes or no answers.

For example, "Am I in a Christmas song?" or "Am I one of Santa's reindeer?" If the answer to any question is no, it's the next player's turn.

4. The winner is the first player to guess who they are. Keep playing until everyone finds out which famous Christmas character they are.

PERISCOPE PUZZLER

You are part of an underwater mission to gain intelligence about an evil genius called The Puzzler who has set up headquarters on Jigsaw Island. You are in submarine 1 and took photograph C of the island using a periscope—a device that lets you see above water. Three other submarines have sent you their photos. Can you work out which submarine took which photo of the island in order to identify the exact location of each one before reporting back to base? Check your answers on page 95.

You use your periscope to zoom in on a jigsaw The Puzzler is working on. Can you figure out which of the pieces are needed to complete the jigsaw? What does the completed puzzle tell you?

CHRISTMAS OBSTACLE COURSE

After all that Christmas dinner it's time for some exercise. Head outside to the garden—or the park—and work off some of that delicious food.

CHRISTMAS OBSTACLE COURSE

Set up the obstacle course below in your garden or in the park.

Place six sticks on the ground spaced evenly apart. The sticks between the Start Line stick and the Finish Line stick each represent a Station. All competitors must complete the following tasks at each Station:

Station One: Jump in and out of a ring of string or a hoop 20 times.

Station Two: Players need to get to Station Three by laying newspaper sheets on the ground and stepping on them—if they step on the ground, they have to go back to the Start Line.

Station Three: Put on a party hat and jump on the spot 20 times.

Station Four: Put on an apron and do a cartwheel, then a handstand, then a somersault and run to Station Five.

Station Five: Still wearing the apron, waddle like a penguin to the Finish Line.

Time how long it takes each competitor to complete the course. The fastest to reach the Finish Line wins.

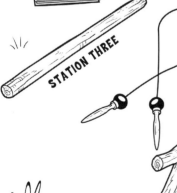

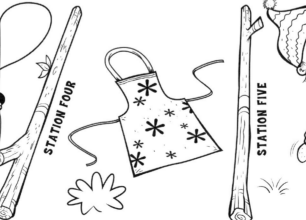

70

FREEZE TAG

Choose a person to be "It." He or she has to run after the other players and tag them. Once a player is tagged, he or she must become frozen in place and stand with their legs apart, not moving.

Players must stay frozen until another player unfreezes them by crawling between their legs. The game ends when all the players except "It" are frozen. The last person to be frozen becomes "It" for the next round.

SNOWBALL RELAY

Place two sticks roughly 100 ft. apart. Give each player a Christmas stocking—a large sock will do.

Place a bag of "snowballs" (cotton balls) at the far end of the course.

Players have to sprint from one end of the course to the other, grabbing a snowball and stuffing it in their stockings each time they reach the bag of snowballs.

The winning player is the first to reach the finish line with 10 snowballs in his stocking.

SWEETIE SEARCH

Take turns hiding small treasures around your backyard or the park. Candy canes, wrapped sweets, or chocolate coins are good. Using a stopwatch, the "Hider" times the other players for one minute.

The person to find the most sweets in that time wins.

MAKE A SPYSCOPE

Periscopes are special devices used by spies to look around corners without being seen. Tanks and submarines are also fitted with periscopes to enable those inside to see what is around or above them. Find out how to make your own, then use it to spy on your family without being seen.

You Will Need:

- 2 clean, dry cardboard juice cartons
- a marker • scissors
- a ruler • strong tape • 2 small rectangular-shaped mirrors

1. Carefully cut the top off each juice carton.

2. Cut a rectangular shape out of the bottom of a carton, leaving roughly a ¼ in. edge around the sides and bottom of the shape, as shown below.

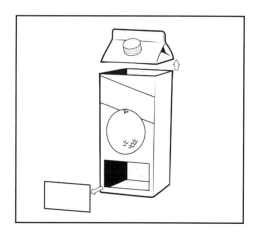

3. Place the carton on its side with the hole facing you. Lay a mirror flat on top of the carton so that its shorter side lines up with the base of the carton.

4. Mark a spot on the carton at the top right-hand and bottom left-hand corners of the mirror with a pen.

5. Remove the mirror and use your ruler to draw a diagonal line between the two dots, as shown.

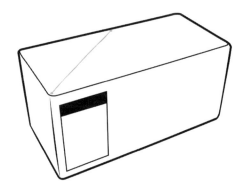

6. Carefully cut along the diagonal line you have drawn.

7. Slide the mirror through the slot that you have made.

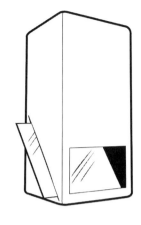

8. Turn the carton around and look through the rectangular-shaped hole in the front of the carton.

You should be able to see the top of the carton in the mirror.

9. Secure the mirror in place using tape.

10. Repeat steps 2 to 9 with the other carton.

11. Turn one of the cartons upside down and place it on top of the other one.

Make sure a rectangular-shaped opening is at the bottom of one carton facing you and the other opening is at the top of the other one and facing away from you.

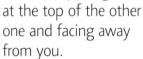

12. Position the cartons so that when you look through the bottom opening, you can see what is ahead of you.

13. Attach the two cartons with tape as shown here.

YOUR SPYSCOPE MISSION

Hold your spyscope horizontally to look around corners, or hold it vertically to look over walls and fences.

You will find that what is ahead of you is reflected in the upper mirror, and then reflected in the lower mirror.

Your Mission: not to be seen.

Time how long you can observe people around you without them seeing you.

If you get spotted, start the clock again. Make notes on what your targets are doing while you spy on them.

SURPRISE!

It's time to unwrap some puzzling presents.
Check your answers on page 95.

RIDDLE RUSE

There are three presents hidden in this house.

Solve the riddles to work out where they are hidden.

1. One is hidden behind something that has hands but no arms and a face but no head.

2. One present has been hidden underneath something that contains garden tools, precious stones, and symbols of love.

3. The last present is tucked between the floorboards, beside something that lives if you feed it, but dies if you give it water.

CHRISTMAS GIFTS

You're giving Aunt Betty, Aunt Susan, Aunt Jane, and Aunt Mary each a bar of soap and a bottle of bubble bath.

Can you draw two straight lines to divide the presents so that each section has a bar of soap and a bottle of bubble bath in it?

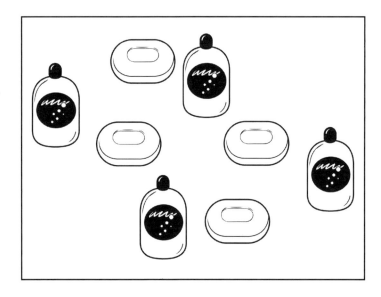

PICKING PRESENTS

Each of these circles represents a type of present. The letters represent the people you need to buy presents for.

Where the circles cross over one another, you could buy more than one type of present for the person inside. For example, *D* likes sports and books, but doesn't like perfume or computer games.

Can you work out who likes perfume, sports, and computer games but does not like books? Who could you buy a book or a computer game for but not perfume or something sporty?

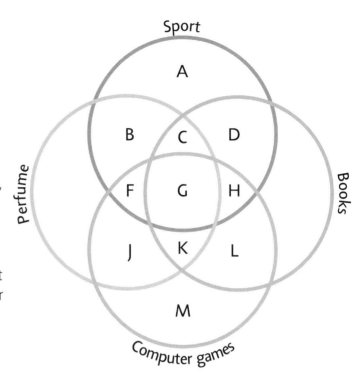

CONNECT THE DOTS

Connect the dots in the correct order to see what Jim was given for Christmas.

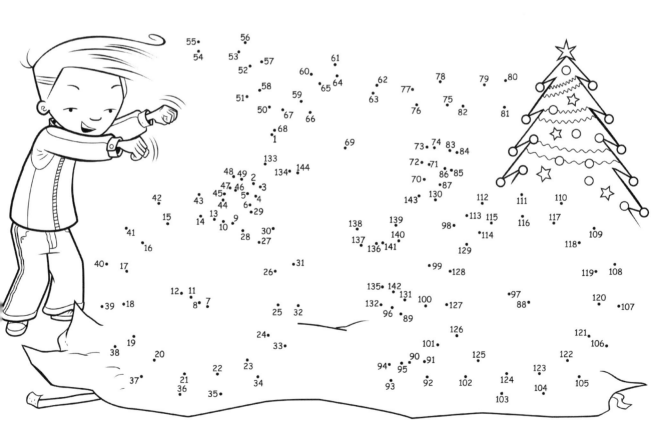

75

CAN YOU SAVE THE DAY?

Help! Nasty Nemesis and his Ugly Crew have stolen gold from the bank. A superhero is needed to solve the problems and save the day. Have you got what it takes? Tackle these puzzles to find out, then check your answers on page 95.

ON THE RUN

Follow the movements of the Ugly Crew to see where they ended up.

They came out of the bank and turned right. They took a left at the corner, then took the first left down a street. They turned right at the corner, then left at the next corner.

They took the third road to the right, then turned right. They then turned right again into a house. Did they run into house A, B or C?

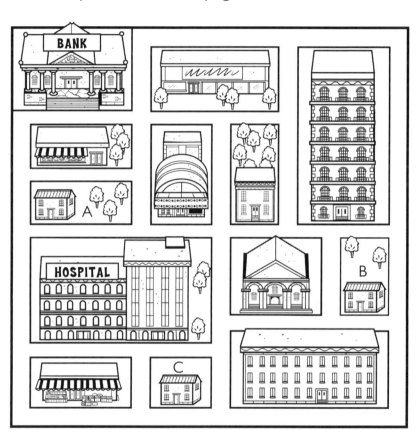

CODE CRACKER

By the time you arrive at the house, the gang is gone, but you find a safe and the gold's inside. Can you crack the code to find the secret combination that will open the safe? (**Clue:** Nasty Nemesis isn't very smart and has used his own name to lock it.)

A	B	C	D	E	F	G	H	I	J	K	L	M
1	2	3	4	5	6	7	8	9	10	11	12	13
N	O	P	Q	R	S	T	U	V	W	X	Y	Z
14	15	16	17	18	19	20	21	22	23	24	25	26

TREASURE TRICKS

Inside the safe you find half the stolen gold and a piece of paper with the numbers below on it. Can you crack the code to find out where the rest of the gold is hidden?
(**Clue:** Each number represents a letter of the alphabet.)

2, 21, 18, 9, 5, 4 / 21 ,14, 4, 5, 18 / 20, 18, 5, 5 / 14, 5, 24, 20 / 20, 15 / 8, 15, 19, 16, 9, 20, 1, 12

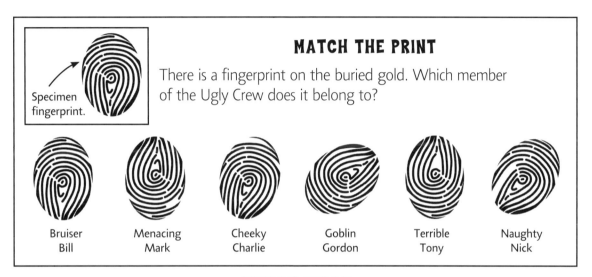

MATCH THE PRINT

There is a fingerprint on the buried gold. Which member of the Ugly Crew does it belong to?

Specimen fingerprint.

| Bruiser Bill | Menacing Mark | Cheeky Charlie | Goblin Gordon | Terrible Tony | Naughty Nick |

PRISON CELLS

You have captured three members of the Ugly Crew and thrown them into prison. The guards have asked you to keep a close eye on them in case they try to escape. Can you write down the coordinates (the letter of the column and the number of the row) of the three squares that have their prison numbers inside?

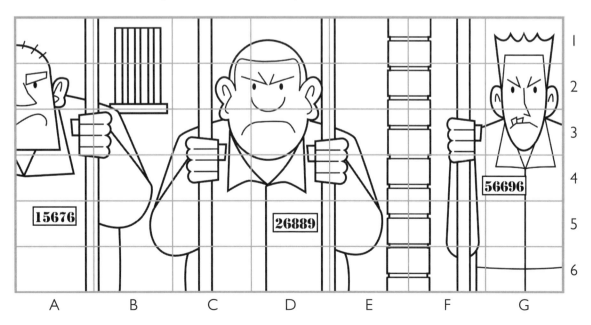

CHRISTMAS BINGO

Be the best at Bingo this Christmas.

HOW TO PLAY

1. This game needs three players. Once you have found three people who are up for the challenge, choose who is going to be the "Caller." The other two players are the "Santas."

2. Cut out the sacks and all the item counters on the opposite page.

3. One Santa takes the holly counters and the holly sack. The other has the Christmas tree counters and Christmas tree sack.

4. Without letting the Caller see, the Santas must then choose six counters and put them face up on their sack game board.

The Santas must keep their boards hidden from the Caller throughout the game.

5. The Caller chooses one of the presents on the list below, and says, for example, "Take out the skateboard." If either or both Santas have the skateboard on their sack game board, they hand it to the Caller.

6. The Caller continues in this way, choosing presents from the list in any order, until one of the Santas has emptied his sack.

7. The first Santa with no presents left shouts "BINGO!" to win the game.

LIST OF ITEMS

1. Socks
2. Cookbook
3. Skateboard
4. Soap
5. Toy airplane
6. Camera
7. Football
8. Tie
9. Toy car
10. Bubble bath
11. Juggling balls
12. Shirt

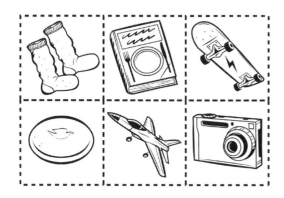

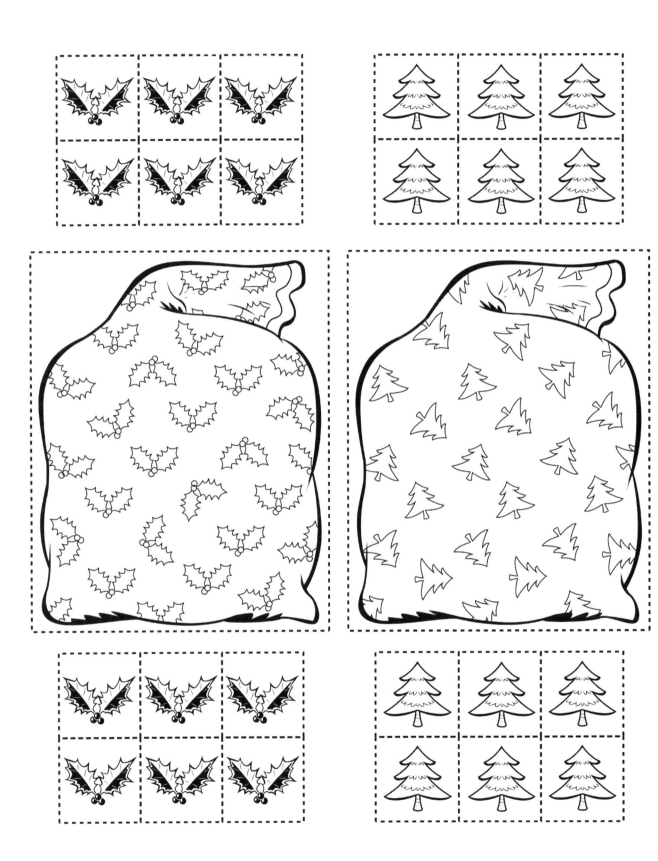

THE POWER OF CHRISTMAS

This is the true story of a short period of
peace during the First World War.

Much of the First World War was fought on battlefields in France and Belgium in a fighting zone known as the Western Front. Fighting the Germans, among other countries, were thousands of British soldiers. Soldiers on each side fired at one another from huge trenches dug into the ground.

On Christmas Eve, 1914, three months after the war started, dusk was beginning to fall in the trenches. For the first time since the war had begun, it became quiet.

Very carefully, the British troops looked out across the area of land known as "no man's land"—a cratered wasteland between the trenches. To their amazement, candles started to appear on Christmas trees on the German side. Singing then rang out into the frosty night in German and in English.

Christmas Day dawned in thick, freezing fog. Voices from both sides began calling out across no man's land, wishing a Merry Christmas to soldiers that had been their bitter enemies.

Gradually, in different places along the Western Front, soldiers stood up in plain sight, waving and calling to the enemy side.

It wasn't long before British and German soldiers came out of their trenches, crossed into no man's land, and met their enemies face-to-face.

Both sides had been given special Christmas Day rations, including Christmas puddings, beer, and biscuits and they began to swap them as gifts. They even swapped buttons from their uniforms as souvenirs. Enemy soldiers shook hands and talked about their families.

Then someone produced a soccer ball and suggested an international match. For an hour or so the soldiers forgot about fighting and concentrated on playing a game of soccer on the frozen ground of no man's land. They used their army caps as goalposts. Several games were played in different parts of the Western Front. The only recorded score, however, was 3–2 to the Germans.

This unexpected Christmas truce between the British and the Germans on the Western Front continued from Christmas Eve to the morning of December 26 in some places and for several days longer in others. With one or two exceptions, no shots were fired.

Sadly, fighting resumed shortly afterward and the First World War continued until November 1918.

TRUE OR FALSE? YOU DECIDE!

How knowledgable are the people around your Christmas dinner table?
Find out with this true-or-false quiz. Check the answers on page 96.

TRUE OR FALSE?

1. A male turkey is called a tom.

2. A traditional Swedish Christmas dinner might include lutefisk—white fish that's been soaked in sodium hydroxide.

3. During the 1660s, when celebrating Christmas was banned in England, it was illegal to eat turkey, goose, duck, or chicken on December 25.

4. In England, Christmas pudding—a steamed dessert made out of fruit—is traditionally soaked in alcohol and set on fire before eating.

5. In Italy, it's traditional to eat roast swan on Christmas Eve.

6. In Russia, it is traditional for some people to fast for 39 days before Christmas Eve.

7. In Portugal, they have an extra feast early on Christmas morning called "consoada." An extra place is laid to remember loved ones who have died.

8. In Canada, it's traditional to roast a whole pig for Nochebuena (the Christmas Eve feast).

9. In Israel, it is tradition to bake bread called the Christmas Braid. The bread is then left on the table until January 6, when it is eaten.

10. In England, Christmas mince pies are made with minced beef.

But I thought Christmas was banned?! Leave me alone!

GO-KART, GO!

To complete this go-kart race, each driver must race to the flag that matches the one on his go-kart. Drivers can drive straight up, down and sideways, but not diagonally across the squares. Only one go-kart can pass through each square. Can you find a route for each go-kart? The first one has been done for you. Turn to page 96 if you get stuck. On your marks, get set, go!

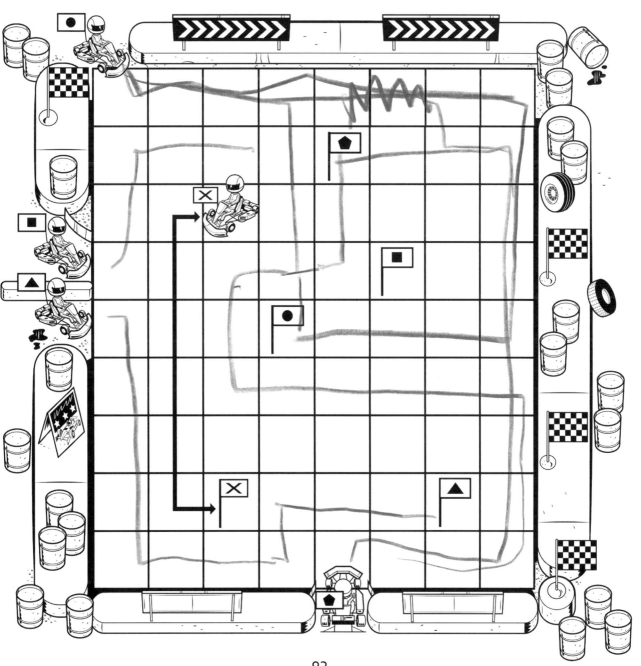

SAY MERRY CHRISTMAS

Wish everyone a Merry Christmas wherever they're from!
A guide to pronouncing the words is written underneath in italics.

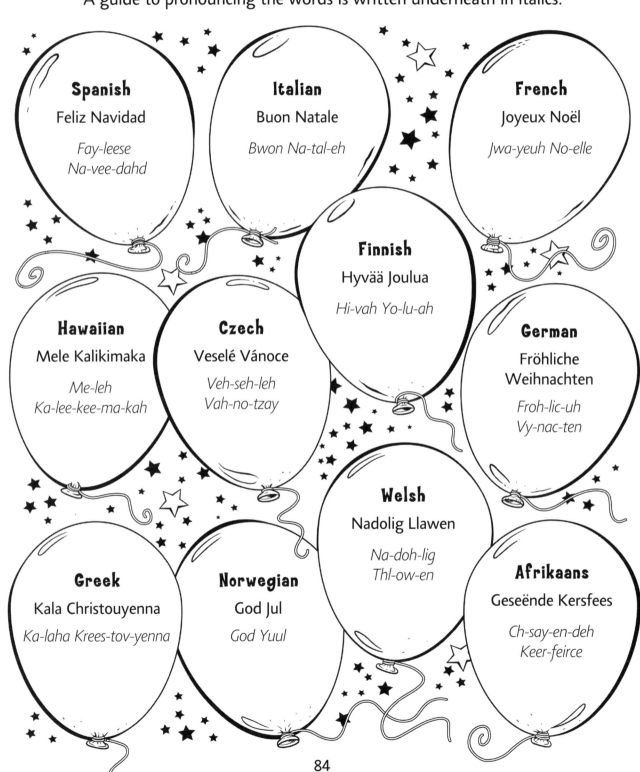

Spanish

Feliz Navidad

*Fay-leese
Na-vee-dahd*

Italian

Buon Natale

Bwon Na-tal-eh

French

Joyeux Noël

Jwa-yeuh No-elle

Finnish

Hyvää Joulua

Hi-vah Yo-lu-ah

Hawaiian

Mele Kalikimaka

*Me-leh
Ka-lee-kee-ma-kah*

Czech

Veselé Vánoce

*Veh-seh-leh
Vah-no-tzay*

German

Fröhliche
Weihnachten

*Froh-lic-uh
Vy-nac-ten*

Welsh

Nadolig Llawen

*Na-doh-lig
Thl-ow-en*

Greek

Kala Christouyenna

Ka-laha Krees-tov-yenna

Norwegian

God Jul

God Yuul

Afrikaans

Geseënde Kersfees

*Ch-say-en-deh
Keer-feirce*

Create your own prizewinning ice sculpture.

WHAT'S YOUR ULTIMATE SUPERPOWER?

Which is better, being invisible or having X-ray vision? Being able to predict the future or having laser eyes? Decide for yourself with this superduper superpower decider!

1. Think of four superpowers that you would love to have and write one inside each of the fireballs on the first row.

2. Decide which of each pair you think would be the most fun to have and write the answers in the fireballs on the second row.

3. Finally, decide which of these two would be your ultimate superpower and write it in the fireball on the last row.

ULTIMATE SUPERPOWER

Cover the rocks with creepy-crawlies.

SEASONAL SCRAPS

Keep a scrapbook record of your Christmas. Cut out pictures and messages from Christmas cards, add labels, tags, and pieces of gift wrap from your gifts, and draw pictures of the funniest festive moments.

ALL THE ANSWERS

CHRISTMAS WORLD
page 5

Fact 9 isn't true. Children in Great Britain hang stockings from fireplace mantelpieces or at the end of their bed.

WINTER RACES
pages 6 and 7

This is Charlie:

B and E are the identical skiers. Bobsled C.

FESTIVE FAMILY FUN
pages 8 and 9

1. C 2. C 3. A 4. B 5. D 6. B 7. B 8. C 9. D 10. C 11. D 12. A

CANDY CANE GAME
page 11

RIDE ON
pages 12 and 13

A. 4 skaters have backpacks on.
B. 5 skaters are completely in the air.
C. 3 skaters have one arm in the air and have both feet on their skateboards.
D. 3 skaters have crash-landed.

Jim would have to land on this square marked with an X:

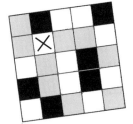

Skater **1**'s wallet is:

Skater **2**'s wallet is:

Skater **3**'s wallet is:

Skater **4**'s wallet is:

CHRISTMAS CODE-BREAKERS
pages 18 and 19

1. MOUNTAIN BIKE
2. GAME CONSOLE
3. SKATEBOARD

Clue One: The next clue is hidden at the foot of an evergreen tree.

Clue Two: The next clue can be found in a flower pot.

Clue Three: Your secret present is hidden inside a white pillowcase.

ROBOT INVASION
pages 20 and 21

The code is: 111, 11, 1001, 100

Box C contains all the pieces needed to make the robot.

Robot K can shoot lasers, walk forward and sideways, but can't walk backward.

ELFISH ANTICS
pages 22 and 23

1. C4 **2.** F3 **3.** G9 **4.** G3 **5.** F9 **6.** D2

Elvis the Elf needs all the pieces in Box **C** to build the toy car.

MERRY MAZE
page 25

ANIMAL GAMES
page 28

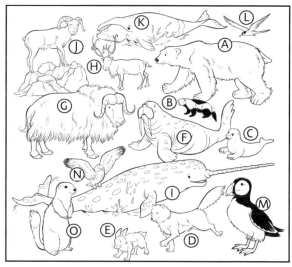

MISSION: SECRET AGENT
pages 30 and 31

Agent's Code Name: Agent Rainstorm.

NORTH POLE PUZZLER
page 26

Polar bears don't eat penguins because they live in completely different parts of the world. Polar bears live in the Arctic, in the far north, while penguins live in the Antarctic, in the far south.

SANTA DASH!
pages 32 and 33

1. D 2. A 3. B 4. E 5. C 6. F

Santa would end up on rooftop **B**.

1. North 2. Woods 3. A hill 4. In the south
5. A skaters' pond 6. Five

COLOSSEUM CONUNDRUMS
pages 34 and 35

The thief is standing up in the first row on the right-hand page, as shown here:

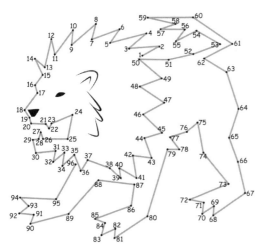

PARTY PUZZLERS
pages 36 and 37

Hat **C** is the odd hat out.

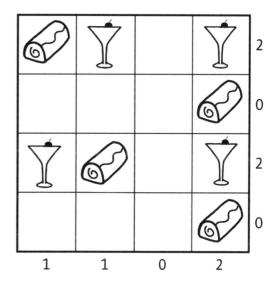

UNTANGLE THE LIGHTS
page 40

Plug **C** is connected to the broken bulb.

TRICKY TREES
page 49

MOUNTAIN OF DOOM
page 51

SNOW-DOKU
page 59

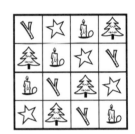

FLY TRAP
page 62

Spider **1** has trapped fly **C**.
Spider **2** has trapped fly **D**.
Spider **3** has trapped fly **B**.
Spider **4** has trapped fly **A**.

FOOD GLORIOUS FOOD
pages 64 and 65

1. B **2.** E **3.** F **4.** A **5.** C **6.** D

You bought some meat, then some cheese, then some bread.

With the change, you could buy **twelve chocolate bars**. OR: You could buy one cookie, two candy canes, eight gum drops, and **nine chocolate bars**.

PERISCOPE PUZZLER
pages 68 and 69

Submarine **2** took picture **D**.
Submarine **3** took picture **A**.
Submarine **4** took picture **B**.

A, **B**, **E** and **H** are the missing jigsaw pieces.

The Puzzler's pirate ship is coming towards the submarine, which tells you that you need to make a quick getaway!

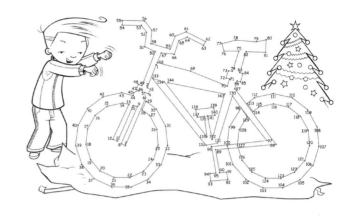

CAN YOU SAVE THE DAY?
pages 76 and 77

The Ugly Crew ended up in house **B**.

The code for the safe is:
Nasty Nemesis: 14, 1, 19, 20, 25 /
14, 5, 13, 5, 19, 9, 19

The gold is "buried under tree, next to hospital."

Goblin Gordon's print was found on the gold.

The robbers' prison numbers are in the following squares: **A5**, **D5**, and **G4**.

SURPRISE!
pages 74 and 75

1. Behind the clock **2.** Under the pack of cards **3.** Beside the fireplace

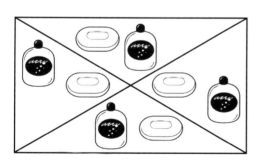

You are picking presents for person **F** and person **L**.

TRUE OR FALSE? YOU DECIDE!
page 82

1. True

2. True

3. False—Christmas was banned, but it wasn't illegal to eat poultry December 25

4. True

5. False—in Italy, it's traditional to celebrate on Christmas Eve with a feast of seven types of fish

6. True

7. True

8. False—this tradition is enjoyed in Cuba

9. False—Christmas Braid bread or "kolach" is a Ukrainian treat

10. False—they are made with fruit, but in the Middle Ages, some people mixed meat in, too

GO-KART GO!
page 83

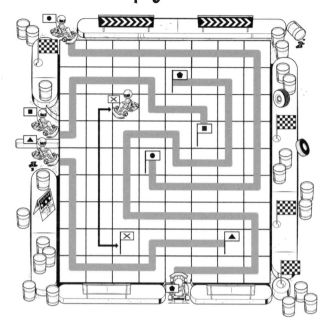